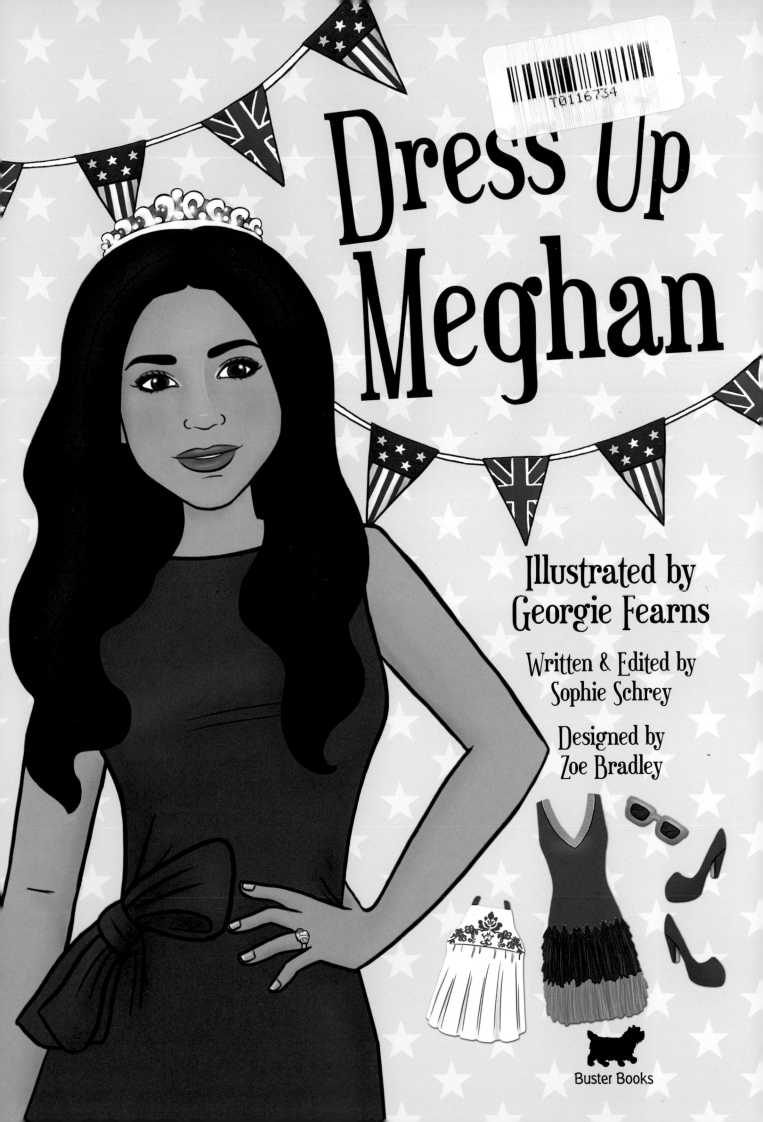

Dress Up Meghan

Illustrated by
Georgie Fearns

Written & Edited by
Sophie Schrey

Designed by
Zoe Bradley

Buster Books

Contents

First published in Great Britain in 2018 by Buster Books, an imprint of
Michael O'Mara Books Limited, 9 Lion Yard, Tremadoc Road, London SW4 7NQ

W www.mombooks.com/buster　F Buster Books　T @BusterBooks

ISBN: 978-1-78055-579-9

2 4 6 8 10 9 7 5 3 1

This book was printed in July 2018 by Ruho Corporation Sdn. Bhd., 334 Sungai Puyu, 13020 Butterworth, Penang, Malaysia.

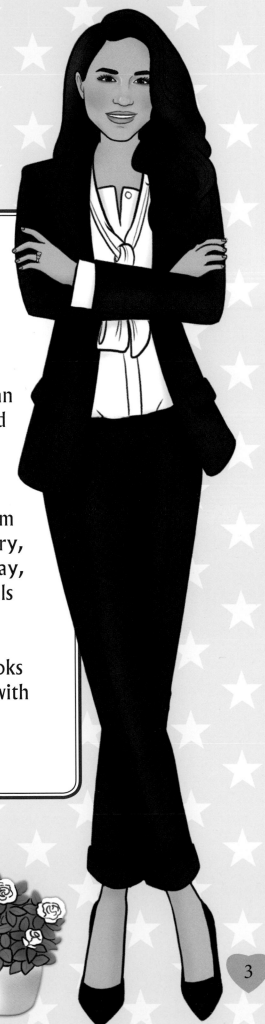

It's Time To Dress Up Meghan

Radiant, creative and ever so chic, Meghan Markle is the royal of the moment – and everyone wants to know what she'll be wearing next.

Now you can be her personal stylist. From the wedding of Meghan to her Prince Harry, to red-carpet looks and a wild safari holiday, dress up Meghan, friends and other royals for every occasion.

With over 600 stickers, recreate iconic looks or mix and match the outfits to come up with your own unique styles.

#Meg4Harry

A Royal Engagement

Harry popped the question over a roast chicken dinner and Meghan said, "YES!" Dress these royal lovebirds for their super-stylish engagement photo shoots.

Meghan's Look

Wherever she is, Meghan never fails to step out in style. Mix and match outfits to create looks for all occasions – from dog walking to street chic.

Merry Christmas

It's Christmas Day and Meghan is joining the Royal Family for their annual appearance at Sandringham. Finish their festive looks with smart outfits and jazzy hats.

A Glitzy Gala

It's a star-studded red carpet at this gala in New York City.
Meghan, Kate, Pippa and Cara are stealing the spotlight.
Dress them to impress in show-stopping outfits.

On Safari

There's only one true king of the jungle in
Meghan's eyes ... and he doesn't have a mane.
Kit them out and finish the safari scene.

Hall Of Fame

Meghan knows how to dress for any big occasion. Complete some of her signature looks from the red carpet.

14

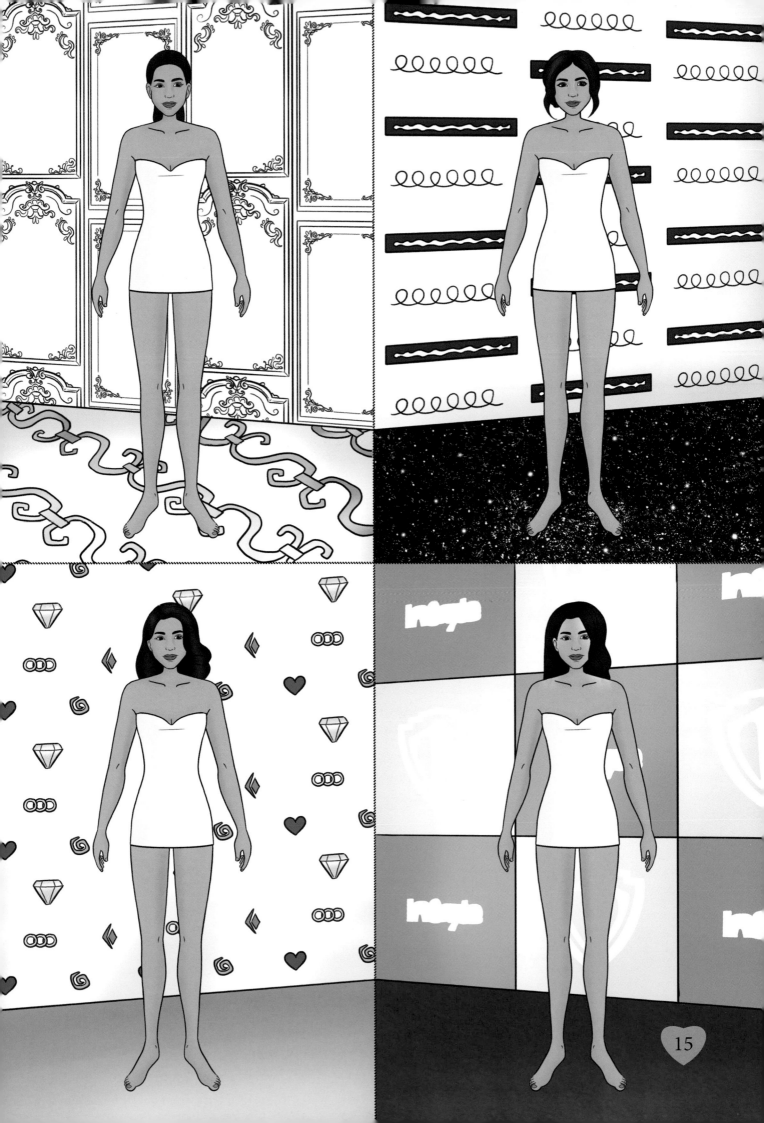

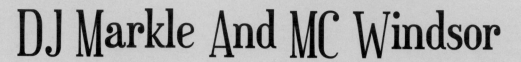

DJ Markle And MC Windsor

Meghan and Harry are mixing it up with a royal visit to a London music station. Dress them up for a day on the decks.

Road Trip

A carefree Californian road trip does wonders for the soul. Complete the chilled vibes with groovy stickers.

Friends Ahoy

Meghan's spending some much-needed 'girl time' with her pals on a sunny Mediterranean cruise. Complete their sizzling summer style with beach outfits and fun accessories.

Royal Wedding

The big day has finally arrived. Meghan has married her prince charming at Windsor Castle and the nation is beaming with joy. But the big question is, what did she wear? You decide!

At Home

The newlyweds are on cloud nine, but they're exhausted from all the excitement of their wedding day. It's time to chill out at home and to relive their special day through their hashtag, #Meg4Harry. Dress them in comfy loungewear and complete their cosy cottage.

... and they lived
happily ever after.

Look 1

Look 2

Look 4

Pages
6 – 7

Look 3

Meghan's hat

Meghan's coat

Meghan's bag & boots

Pages 8 – 9

Kate's tights

Kate's coat & accessories

Beatrice's hat

Camilla's hat

Eugenie's hat

Queen's brooch

Queen's hat

William's bow tie

Harry's bow tie

Meghan's shoes

Meghan's outfit

Kate's dress

Pages 10 – 11

Pippa's dress & shoes

Cara Delevingne's outfit

Pages
12 – 13

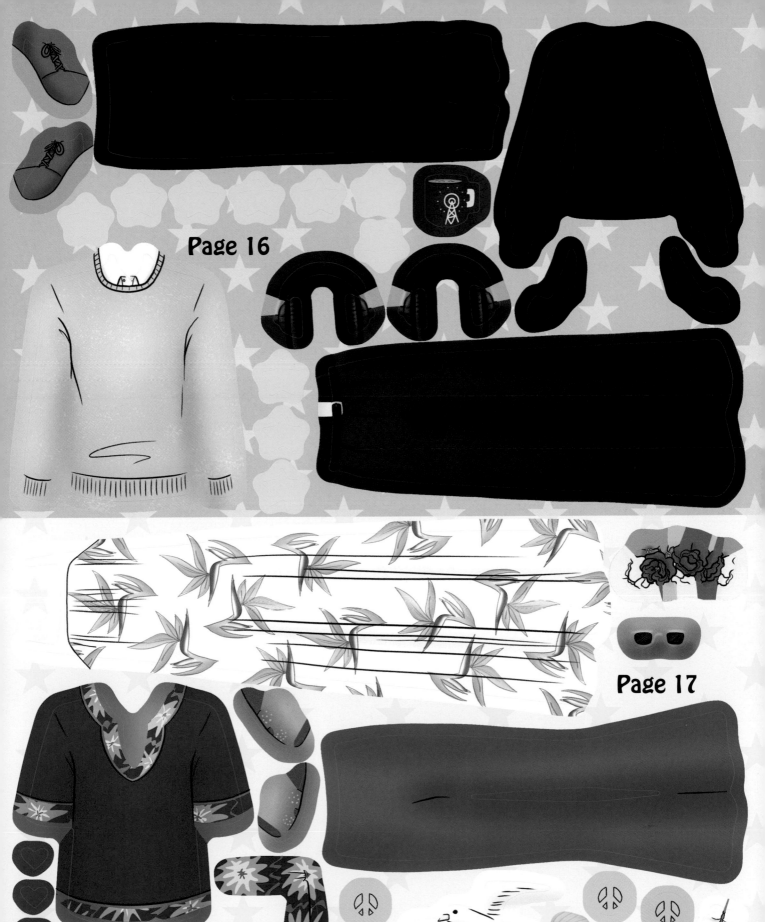

Page 16

Page 17

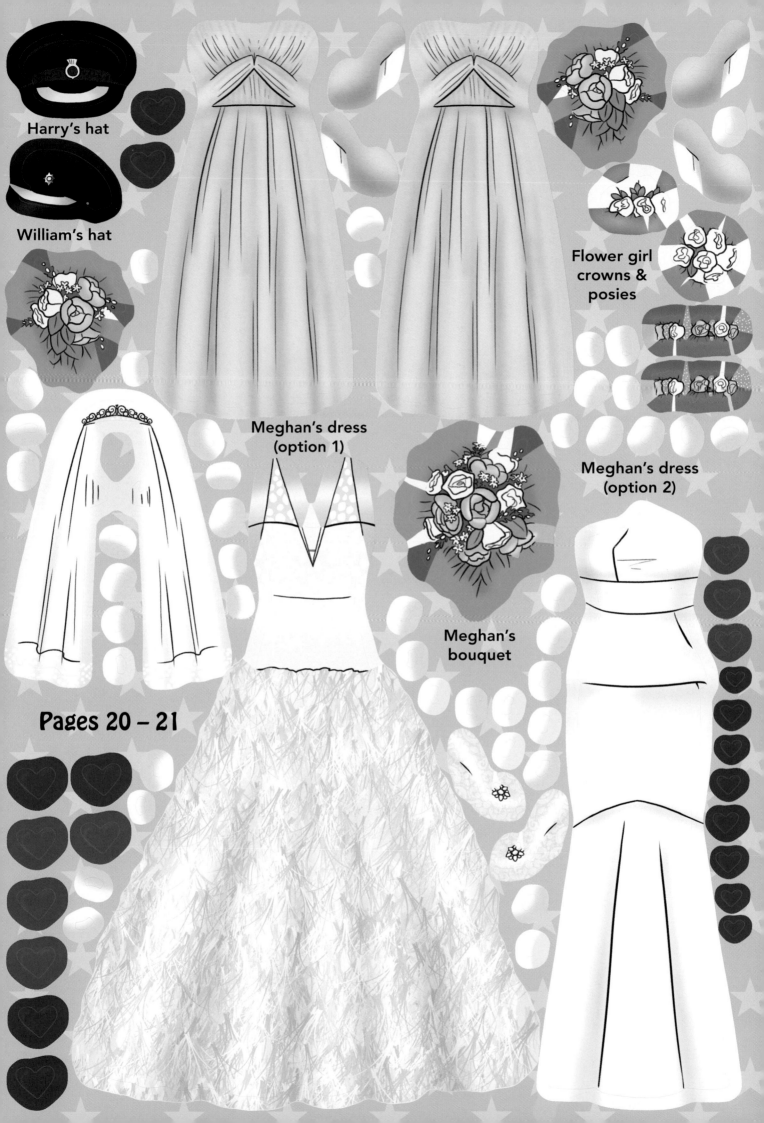

Harry's hat

William's hat

Flower girl
crowns &
posies

Meghan's dress
(option 1)

Meghan's dress
(option 2)

Meghan's
bouquet

Pages 20 – 21

Pages 22 – 23

Page 24